Walking With Jesus

Jane Wyman

Walking With Jesus

Jane Wyman

Copyright © 2025 by Jane Wyman

All rights reserved.

Published by Red Penguin Books

Bellerose Village, New York

ISBN

Print 978-1-63777-805-0

Digital 978-1-63777-804-3

No part of this book may be reproduced in any form or by any electronic or mechanical means, including information storage and retrieval systems, without written permission from the author, except for the use of brief quotations in a book review.

This, I Know

I walked into the church
There sitting in the corner
Was a little waif
Her clothes were askew
Her hair all uncombed
She was singing,
Jesus Loves me
over and over again.
Her smile was from ear to ear
I needed no sermon that day.
The song was in her heart
And she was singing like a canary
Jesus loves me, This I know,
For the bible tells me so.
This is faith.
I turned around and went home.

~ Jane Wyman

*This book is dedicated to my grandmother
Edith Richter,
to Joyce C Woods who always believed in me
and to Linda Trott Dickman, Poet, Teacher,
Mentor, Friend and who was pivotal in having
this book published.*

Contents

Foreword	xi
Who is God?	1
Good Morning God	2
Rays Of Sunshine	3
Morning Ritual	4
His Guidance	5
Passing Seasons	6
God's Handiwork	7
The Monarch	8
Raindrops	9
The Celebration of Life	10
Music of Nature	11
Welcome, Fall!	12
The Master Artist	13
A Fall Scene	14
The Bounty	15
Ye Olde Pot	16
Walking	18
Reach Up	19
The World Is Spinning	20
Alone	21
The Star Shone Bright	22
Jesus	23
Sleep Baby Jesus	24
Christmas	25
Born a King: A Litany	26
This is Christmas	27
Where Is Jesus	28
Redemption	29
My Savior	30
Hallelujah	31
Gather round my children	32

Rain	33
A Rose	34
The Weeping Willow Tree	35
A Dogwood Tree	36
Reflective Moon	37
Are You, Angry Lord?	38
Raindrops	39
Coping With Life	40
A Late Night Prayer	42
Whitecaps	44
Hold Me	45
Gifts	46
Enjoy His Gift	47
My Sanctuary	48
Rest and Relaxation	49
The Junkyard Dog	50
The Humble Life	51
Temptation	53
Peace	54
Resurrection Day	55
He Lives	56
Listen	57
Parades and Patriotism	58
Changing Seasons	59
Heavenly Blessings	60
Slow Roll	61
Soaring	62
Storm Clouds	63
Let Him In	64
Lord Walk With Us	65
Walking Together	66
Together We Walk	67
Your Decision	68
About the Author	71

Foreword
by Linda Trott Dickman

Jane Wyman used to describe herself to me as "The Head of a Single Household." She would announce it proudly. Jane started working at the age of 18 and contributed to her family's income from then until she was the only one left. She cooked and cleaned for grandparents while working, full time. She has lived many lives. When she encountered Jesus, everything changed.

This book represents Jane's journey and the answer to a prayer, where she just wants all to see and know the beauty of God's world. The wonder of falling snow, birds winging their way south, the face of a single flower.

Won't you take this journey? It is often raw and unapologetic. She hopes that it helps people who read it to know that they are never alone. Jesus is always with them.

May the Lord bless you as you join Jane on this walk through God's world. Jane, daughter of the King, precious child of God.

Linda Trott Dickman

Who is God?

He is the face of a newborn child
A quiet whisper answering as you call out
The hand that holds yours when you are lonely
The roaring sound of the waterfalls
The quiet babbling of a small brook
The smile on a person's face asking if they can help you
A crimson tree standing majestically tall
As its leafy arms spread for birds
Rain that quietly falls
White capped mountains rising royally

He is the sun rising each day
The snow quietly falling in the night leaving a blanket of white
The beauty of a stark, barren silhouette of a bare tree against the snow
The first buds of spring
A flower bed of red, white, and yellow flowers blooming
The hummingbird drinking from a flower
Yellow, white, and orange butterflies on the wing

God is all of this and more
Listen, hear Him speaking

Good Morning God

Good morning, God
As I open my eyes
I thank you for the sun
shining brightly in the sky
I thank you for the flowers
that come into each of our lives
for the wind that refreshes
I thank you for the rain
that brings life to the earth
Dear God, thank you for everything

Rays Of Sunshine

In the silence of the morning
as the sun is shining through the trees
I love to listen to the birds

chirp

chirp

chirping

They seem as if they are saying
Rise up and live the day
that God gave us all
to live fully in every way

Morning Ritual

Up in the morning
look into the mirror
shudder at what you see
Off to the shower
and a miracle worker you be

Dry the hair
rub it briskly
and then get out the mousse
jump into my clothes quickly

To work, to work
the wind blowing, the snow falling
and start all over
to fix my crowning glory

Oh well! Better hair day tomorrow

His Guidance

In the early morning hours
before the sun is up
I like to sit and meditate
with coffee in my cup

To thank God for the day
and ask for His guidance
for each and every step I take
as I plod along my way

I feel His peaceful presence
as together we walk side by side
doing life's daily tasks
and letting Him be my guide

Passing Seasons

Summer, fall, winter, spring
Seasons passing day by day
We are so busy in life
We don't take time to pray

Each season has its glories
To behold and live and play
Sunrise and sunset
Gone, another day

Enjoy nature's beauty
Each leaf as it flutters by
Snow flakes will soon fall
And winter draweth nigh

When you go to the park
Take a picnic lunch and stay
Enjoy the beauties in nature
And dine your time away

God's Handiwork

"Twas God's hand that showered
Over this beautiful wintery land
And surrounded everyone
With His dazzling white hand

The evergreens standing tall
Cloaked in their sparkling white gown
Shouting praises to God
Each one wearing a crown

When I bow my head in prayer
I always thank you, Father
For clothing us in love
Singing praises of our own

The Monarch

One lone butterfly
flits among the flowers
lands here and there
and rests for a little while

So fragile and delicate
his little wings they be
he catches the updraft
and on his way he goes

Thank you butterfly
for sharing a blink with me
and looking in the eyes of God
His beauty we may see

Raindrops

I love to sit in nature
count the raindrops as they fall
each one a little blessing
then my troubles seem so small

Each raindrop is a gift from God
to bring us cheerful flowers
brighten our mundane day
show us His mighty power

When you encounter raindrops
if your day is dark and dreary
just count the little raindrops
turn your dreary into cheery

The Celebration of Life

Rise up!
Oh, women of Christian Faith
Celebrate! Each day,
Celebrate! Each minute
For yesterday is gone
Tomorrow may never be ours
Live each day
Love each day
For this is!

The Celebration of Life

Music of Nature

Ah!
The sounds of nature
Birds chirping in the trees
Rambling brooks rushing over rocks
Geese flying in V formation
Honking on their way
Squirrels chattering
Trees rustling in the wind
All this is the Music of Nature
Given to us by God.

Welcome, Fall!

The geese are flying south
The pumpkin's wearing frost
The air is getting chilly
The shopping list all crossed

Thanksgiving is just ahead
With turkey, stuffing, sweets and pie
All ready for the feast
And friends and family stopping by

As we are seated at the table
With family all around
Take time to thank God
In His blessings we abound

The Master Artist

The leaves quietly fall down
The sun sets a little earlier
Fall is on its way
colorful bounty abundant
This is God's painting
orange, red, yellow, and crimson leaves fall
all for us to behold
Enjoy the beautiful painting in nature
This is our canvas, placed here by God
for you

A Fall Scene

What a glorious day it is today
to be out and about the park
to listen to the honking of the geese
as they fly overhead

To enjoy all the beautiful things
God has given us to see
Rest our weary bones
as we sit for a spell and chat

Life is such a fast pace
we need time to refresh
What better way to reflect
than sharing time in God's creation!

The Bounty

The frost is on the pumpkin
The geese are flying south
The air is getting chilly
With all good things to come

Thanksgiving is just ahead
With turkey, stuffing, sweets, and pie
All ready for the feast
And friends and family stopping by

As we are seated at the table
With family all around
We take time to thank God
For all the blessings in Him abound

Ye Olde Pot

Sitting up there on the shelf
In an out-of-the-way spot
With a smile on its side
Is an old metal soup pot

My mother used to stir and stir
that old soup pot each day
To make delicious meals for us
And send us on our way

We were an even dozen
Seated around the table
We said grace and then dug in
Even little Mabel

For your see, in older days
Meat was rationed for the poor
Mother used bone and broth
Vegetables from our store

Just think of all the hungry souls
That precious pot has fed
With a soup bone and veggies
And nothing else but bread

The meal complete, our tummies full
We cleaned our bowls each night
We all grinned from ear to ear
Not a speck of food in sight

Ye Olde Pot

Our soup pot held our secrets
They were seasoned oh so well
Each meal a new memory
Tasty soup and a smile

Walking

Hey God! Here I am
Ready for the day
To walk each step along the way
With You by my side

With my hand in Yours
To live each moment in life
Hopefully, avoiding the strife
We wrestle the problems

Be patient with me, God
A babe is what I am
And You the blessed Lamb
I can take one step at a time

Together we will walk
I will take Your lead
I will take Your speed
You my faithful guide

Reach Up

If you're stressed, reach up
If you're sad, reach up
If you're lonely, reach up
God's waiting to take your hand.

The World Is Spinning

I feel lost! How about you?
The world is spinning too fast
The holidays are coming
Demands are overwhelming
Christmas presents to buy
Parties to attend
Here I stand alone in a crowd
Have you ever felt like that?

People all around
All caught in a whirlwind
We need to

Stop!

Talk to our Creator
Lay our problems on Him
Share any joys, our sorrows
Jesus is always willing to listen

Alone

It is Christmas Eve
Here I sit alone at home
Church is closed due to Covid
Christmas music plays on the radio
It's silent in my head

I see stars
I see the manger in Bethlehem
Mary and Joseph
Kneeling beside the baby
Hallelujah, the King is born

The Star Shone Bright

The cherubs are singing
The lights are twinkling
Peace is upon the earth
The baby is lying in a manger

The stable is quiet
The baby sleeps soundly
The wise men saw the star
and are making their way to Jesus

Gifts they bring– gold, frankincense, and myrrh
to the baby in a manger
The greatest gift on earth
given by God to us

Jesus

My precious baby,
As I sit holding you in my arms
It is hard to realize You have been
born my Savior
So small and innocent You are
a Savior to all the world.

I am so humbled
that God chose me, Mary, to birth you,
to nurture You for a short while
until You will be about your Father's business
Then you will be a carpenter, teacher,
preacher, and our Savior
Following your father's calling
For now, You are my precious baby Jesus.

Sleep Baby Jesus

Sleep baby Jesus
As in your manger you lay
Come to Earth to save us
Born this Christmas Day

Hallelujah, the angels are singing
And heralding your birth
For unto us in Bethlehem
Our Savior has come to earth

Sleep baby Jesus
For soon your journey begins
From the manger in Bethlehem
To Calvary, our vict'ry to win

Christmas

Christmas! What is it to you? Do you run
around helter-skelter shopping, baking,
cleaning, working overtime, partying? When
do you take time out for Jesus? The babe in
a manger—the reason for Christmas.
Without Jesus' birth
there would be no Christmas.

Born a King: A Litany

The child of a virgin:
>He was born a King

Mary and Joseph knelt beside Him:
>He was born a King

Laid Jesus in a manger in swaddling cloth:
>He was born a King

The angels hovered over Jesus:
>He was born a King

A heavenly glow encircled Jesus' head:
>He was born a King

The world's Savior in a manger:
>He was born a king

Receive this Savior:
>He was born a King

This is Christmas

The brightest star ever
Shone over a humble stable
In Bethlehem of Judea
Where baby Jesus was born
On this blessed Christmas morn.

His mother Mary
Wrapped him in swaddling clothes
Laid him in a manger.
A humble beginning for our Savior
Wise men followed the star
To see the newborn babe
Bearing gifts of gold, frankincense, and myrrh.

This is Christmas!

Where Is Jesus

The lights have dimmed
The trees are gone
Cookies all eaten
Relatives have all gone home
Christmas presents returned
Decorations all put away
Christmas is over, and the world marches on
The manger put neatly in a box

BUT WHERE IS JESUS?

Is He in your heart forever?
Does he walk beside you every day?

Keep JESUS in your heart
Your step will be lighter
Your journey will be richer

Redemption

It's amazing, it's wonderful
The son of God was born
In a lowly stable in Bethlehem
And laid to rest in a manger

He came to Earth to save us
From sin's almighty hold
To walk each day through life
And bring renewal to our soul

Rejoice, oh Christian brothers
Today, our sin is lifted
As we walk day by day
With our hand in His

When you are down and out
Fall on your knees
Pray to God Almighty
For the precious gift of His son

Rejoice, Oh Christian Brothers!

My Savior

Jesus, my Savior,
Jesus, my friend,
Jesus, you died for me
To wash away all my sins
I fall to my knees and pray

Hallelujah

Hallelujah Hallelujah
Christ arose
From the grave to victory
Forevermore to reign
And set all sinners free

HALLELUJAH!

Gather round my children

The thunder roars
The lightning strikes
And flashes to the earth
The crowd moves around
Suddenly, in the form of a lightning strike
Jesus is standing among us

Gather round, my children
Listen to my story
How I died on the cross
So all could be in glory
I carried all your sins
On my shoulders on the cross
That everyone could be with me
In all eternity

My brothers and sisters
As you walk along your way
Keep me by your side
With me you will abide

Rain

It's raining out
Let the rain hit your nose
Run between the drops
And squish mud between your toes.

Enjoy the silly game
When the rain falls so hard
Just run around and play
As each raindrop falls in your yard.

Come play with me
Come play with me
We'll run in all the puddles
And see what we can see.

A Rose

I have a rose brightly blooming in my yard
A rose that needs tender loving care
It is so delicate
And needs special care

This rose scars easily if violated
And can be prickly at times
This rose likes company
When you look deeply at the center of this rose
You will see a much softer pink

The rose is the most lovable flower I have ever known
The Rose is my Grandfather.

The Weeping Willow Tree

Under the weeping willow tree
As we sit here, just you and me
Watching the world go running by
Under the weeping willow tree

Many a bird has trilled his call
Sitting on the old willow tree
Many animals have sheltered safe
Under the weeping willow tree

Feast your eyes upon God's masterpiece
The Almightiness of His hand on thee
Join in songs of all people
Under the weeping willow tree

A Dogwood Tree

Upon a wooden cross
Christ was crucified
The nails in his hands
His pierced side
He hung and bled for me

The sky darkened
The heavens roared
The veil was rent in two
When they crucified my Jesus

The agony, the suffering
The whole world's sin He bore
Blood, sweat, and tears
Were on His face
For His redeemed world

He arose from the dead, my Jesus
To reign eternally
The Savior of the world
A gift to all mankind

Reflective Moon

The moon reflects
Across the newly fallen snow
The world is quiet
Trees are bending low
With arms in prayer
And beauty is everywhere

God has taken His palette in hand
And painted us a picture
The moon reflecting the trees
Across the white land

Everything is quiet and peaceful
Not a bird in sight
Just nature all at rest
On this quiet moonlit night

Are You, Angry Lord?

Are You angry with me Lord?
Have I forgotten to pray
Amidst the hustle and bustle
Of this, my busy day

Have I neglected to help
Someone along the way
Whose erring steps are faltering
To show them the way

Forgive me, Lord, for human I am
And sometimes lose my way
But evening hours
I always come to You to pray

To lay my burden down
And rest in Your arms
Until the morning comes
And You give me another day

Raindrops

It is raining
I am sitting under a fishing pier on the beach
Perched in a corner
Listening to the waves
The roaring, booming waves
Rolling in with white foam
They are slamming into the pier, making it shake
And they dissipate all foamy over the sands
I sit quietly
And listen to God's music
Soon, I feel a quietness encompass me
The voice of God is speaking to me through His magnificent call
Powerful waves
The music of heaven
Listen Listen Listen
You will hear it too…

Coping With Life

It's quiet

I walk the halls of my mind
Thinking, thinking
Trying to cope with life
In its ever-changing pattern

Listening to the monotonous sounds
of a house well lived in.
Motors whirring, heaters running
Looking for a hand to grab

I get down on my knees
And start praying
To the only One who cares and
Who is with me at all times

Father, I cry out
Please take my hand
Walk with me through the loneliness
Take my hand
And let me know that I matter
Let me unload my innermost thoughts
And lay them on Your shoulder

Give me the strength for the journey
Peace of mind to deal with today's problems
Quietness in my heart
Take away my anxious feeling

Coping With Life

Father, give me Your peace
That passes all understanding
Let me rest in the shelter of your arms
For without You, I am nothing

When I was younger
I was much stronger for the battle
But now at an advanced age
Life is frightening as I walk step by step
Challenges in every direction
Little things limiting my movement
Financial problems in all directions
Mobility is a problem

Father, I ask that You walk with me
Take my hand and guide me
Let me rest in Your Almighty hand
And triumph every day in my life
Over life's challenges

A Late Night Prayer

Alone in my silence
Floating on the ocean
Nowhere to go
No one to lean on
No one to talk to
My burden is pushing me down

Just drifting
Not being able to cope
Wanting someone to help
But only you, God, can help
At this time

So many things are changing
My life
My age
My ailments
Whether large or small
They are challenging

I don't have the strength
To fight this battle
I need help—someone to listen

I am teetering on the brink
Do I give up and jump?
Do I fight with what little I have left
God, what is my answer?

A Late Night Prayer

I am currently examining how you made me
All the love you put into my body
Now, one of the wires is
short-circuiting and
I am confused

Do I jump?
Do I bail out?
What do I do?
I am having trouble dealing
with the problems of life

So alone
No one to talk to
I can't even feel your hand
In mine
Help me, Father.

Whitecaps

Surf crashing!
Wind blowing in my face!
Water swirling around my feet!
Footprints in the sand as I walk!
God's cathedral!

I find a secluded spot
and meditate
Laying my troubles on God
listening to His music
I am renewed
by the music of the surf …

Hold Me

Covered in your love
I lay asleep
Resting peacefully in your keep
Protected from all harm
As I battle through the storm

Your arms enfold me
Your love secures me tight
While the battle is raging
Throughout the night

Morning comes, I lift myself out
of the shelter of your arms
And hold your hand and continue
To march forward

Knowing at last that when evening falls
Your restful arms will embrace me in my sleep.

Gifts

Lots
To use
For people
To help them walk
To ease their journey
Forward on life's highway
Extending my hand in peace
Guiding them through their daily paths
Lifting up each burden to Jesus
Leaning upon His everlasting arms.

Enjoy His Gift

Take a walk in nature
Feel the wind in your face
Slow down
And enjoy God's amazing grace

Listen to the loon's mournful cry
Watch him bob to and fro
See the diamonds on the water
All nature is at peace

Enjoy each and every day
Our God gives us as a gift
To enjoy the beauty of His handiwork
Slow down, enjoy His gift

My Sanctuary

It is quiet in my sanctuary
The geese come gliding in
Landing on the river
The wind is blowing gently
Across the river still

Be still, my soul
And see the face of God.

Rest and Relaxation

Come down to my secret hiding place
And while away the hours
The sound of nature all around
The waves lapping on the rocks

A pleasant break from the hustle and bustle
Put your phone aside
Simply listen to the sounds of nature
Enjoy the scenic ride

Rest and relax
From the whirlwind of society
Unwind from our hectic life
Tis' nature at its best

The Junkyard Dog

It was snowing hard as I walked down the street.
In front of me was a dog, obviously pregnant
looking for a place to give birth.
As I walked out in front of the local junkyard
The dog slipped into the gate.
She looked very tired and anxious.
She searched for a place to have her baby.
Tucked under a trashed car, she found a blanket
just right to give birth.
Finally, she gave birth to one little boy.
She nursed her baby, and he grew strong.

It was 2000 years ago,
Mary and Joseph walked along the road.
Mary was very weary, and she was about to give birth.
As Mary and Joseph walked,
found a stable with animals behind an Inn.
Sheep, cows, and a donkey all resting in the stable.
Mary found a small corner with clean hay.
Exhausted, Mary lay down and gave birth to a boy child
named Jesus.
After birthing Jesus, Mary nursed Him, laid Him in the
manger.
This child was the Savior of the world,
His birth, as humble as the junkyard pup's.

The Humble Life

You came to us a baby
born in a lowly manger
of ever so humble parents
and Your calling came from your Father

You walked the land for over thirty years
healing many persons on Your way
Your disciples by your side
You taught people on your journey

You rode into Jerusalem
on a donkey so lowly
with palms thrown on the ground
as You went slowly to your death

You were beaten and flogged
and then turned over to Pilate.
One person was to be freed
Barabbas was chosen by the crowd

The throngs said "Crucify him."
and to Your death You would go
up the hill to Golgotha you walked
carrying Your cross on Your shoulders

The sins of the world You carried
on your sinless shoulders
nailed to a cross You would be
and hung there until You gave up Your life

Walking With Jesus

You were buried in a tomb
stayed there for three days
Then you arose
from the grave to the sky
to be with your Father forever
and our Savior always to be

Thank you, Jesus

Temptation

To the desert I must go
As guided by my spirit
For Satan to tempt me
and prove I am the Son of God

My hunger unbearable
Satan came to me
"Said *turn these stones to bread and eat
And hunger no more"*

My answer to Satan:
"*Man does not live by bread alone,
But every word out of the mouth of God"*

Satan still had his agenda
In my weakened state
He took me to the rooftop temple
said" *jump and angels will catch you"*

I merely said, *"Do not tempt God so foolishly."*
Again, he tempted me on a mountain top so high
said "all this will be yours
If only you will bow down and worship me."

Once more, I said, "Worship the Lord God and obey Him only."
Finally, Satan left me and went away
At that time, I continued my forty days and nights
the angels took care of me.

Peace

I spoke to my God in the middle of the night
He said to me, "You are free.
You have come to me on bended knee
I gave my life for thee."

Resurrection Day

Jesus, you were born
In a lowly stable
placed in a manger for a bed
You were destined to be the Savior
to all the world

For 33 years, as you grew
You were a carpenter, teacher,
worker of miracles, healer

You blessed the marriage at Cana, fed the 5000,
performed countless miracles
destined to be the Savior to all the world

Then came your time to fulfill your calling
You rode into Jerusalem on a donkey
with palms strewn in your path
Throngs shouted hallelujah

You were sent to trial, found guilty
to Your death, you would go
the crowd shouted crucify! crucify!

Up to Golgotha, you walked
carrying your own cross
You were nailed to that cross
to the grave You must go

On Easter Sunday, you arose

our Savior forever to be…

He Lives

The day drew dark
The thunder rolled
Lightening flashed
Jesus said, "It is finished."

People cheered, people prayed
The soldiers cast lots for His clothes
But on that fateful day
The Son of God died

They laid Him in a tomb
Wrapped in white cloths and spices
Rolled the stone across the door
And there the Son of God lay.

Early in the morning
The women came to the tomb
The stone was rolled away
Jesus Christ was not there

Hallelujah to the Christ
Hallelujah to the risen Savior
Jesus died, but now lives
To reign forevermore

Listen

You will hear
Taps being played
On this Memorial Day
For all those who gave
Their lives for the Red, White, and Blue

Quietly reflect on our independence.

Parades and Patriotism

I love patriotism and puppy dogs
Summer holidays are special
parades and picnics

My grandfather and I standing
on the corner of Main Street USA
on the 4th of July
Anxiously awaiting the parade
Suddenly, I hear drums and horns
I see Old Glory blowing in the wind
John Phillip Sousa's *Stars and Stripes*
deafening your ear.

Military men dressed in their uniforms,
marching side by side
carrying their appropriate flag
I am proud to be an American
As Old Glory goes by

I also bow my head and remember
those men and women who gave
The ultimate sacrifice for the USA to be free.

    GOD BLESS THE USA

Changing Seasons

The seasons march along
Summer is on the run
The days are getting shorter
The air is turning chilly

Frost will soon be on the pumpkin
The trees are in full color
all the colors of the palette
displayed by the Almighty's hand

The geese have headed south
The squirrels are working hard
The pumpkins are in the field
Waiting for frost

Nature is at rest:

Soon, the snow will come
and cover all the ground
The earth will rest for a season
until spring comes marching in

Heavenly Blessings

Lord, let me wake up each day
to the sun shining on my face
with a smile from ear to ear
for the life You have given me today

Let me walk through the day
holding Your hand
Teach me to have patience
when events arise, I cannot control
Let me know You are with me
by the song a bird sings
by the green shoots coming forth
With all the budding flowers
and through every day
hold my hand all the way
Together we will navigate life

Slow Roll

My soul is being called
To the calm and peaceful water
Where God is in His element
And life moves right along

The tides forever roll
To the ever-changing music
The music of nature
Is peaceful to my soul

I quietly sit and watch
As gulls fly to and fro
And the mighty river keeps rolling
Directed by the hand of God.

Soaring

Have you ever communed with nature
on a quiet sandy beach
watching the sun rise out of the ocean
and beads of water drip off
watched the birds soar to and fro
and dip in for a fish

walk along the beach, leaving footprints
in the sand and watch how long they stay

Life is funny--it comes and it goes, and there is
not enough communing we do

Take time to be with God
any time of day
Take time to be with family, for they are
always on their way

Last but not least;
when you lie down at night
thank God for all the heartfelt
moments in your life

Storm Clouds

I love to sit in my quiet place
And watch the river roll along
The boats swaying at their mooring
And the clouds racing by

Nature in all its glory
Each and every day
Enjoy its many moods
With the wind blowing in your face

The trees are swaying gently
As storm clouds approach
Soon it will be raining
Drops upon your face

Silently, the drops they fall
And refresh our Earth's flowers
Keeping a perfect balance
Of nature's beautiful painting

Let Him In

Does your shoulder sag under
the burden you carry?
Are you weary of the world?
Is life breaking through your walls?

Try praying on your knees!

Do you know your Savior carried your burden
He carried all of your sins
He understands your every thought
and will help you if you only let him in

Try praying on your knees!

Get to know Him
Talk to Jesus as your friend
Listen for Him to answer
He will help you carry your burden

Lord Walk With Us

Lord, as we walk through life
amid the trials and tribulations
Be with us as life closes in
and hold our hand as we
onward travel

We are only given so much time
In the world of changing events
Help us to be guided by
Your loving mercy, to stay right and true

Hear our prayer in the silence
and guide us along the way
that one day we will be
beside You forever more

Walking Together

My friend, I want you to know
I have walked by your side for many a day
I patiently waited for you to call
But you had other priorities

Step by step, we walked along
You never knowing I was there
So concerned you were with life
You had no time for me

Patiently, I still walked with you
Waiting Waiting Waiting
For you to call my name
And we will walk together as one

Together We Walk

You say to me, I love you
You say you are my friend
You say to me, I am special
And will be to the end

We walk along together
As you look into my soul
See the scars that mold me
Keep me from being whole

You never made a mistake
Your road was not easy
You reach out Your hand
To take and guide me, say *I love you*

Day by day, You walk with me
And help me carry my load
You say just one more thing
To each and every one
I will never leave you
Or let you walk alone

Your Decision

My friend, I want you to know
I walk beside you each day

Waiting patiently for you to ask for my help
I am always waiting to help you, but you must ask

You must make a conscious decision to walk with me
For my rules are different than man's

When you make that decision
We will walk hand in hand through life

Each day will be better than the one before
With my help

                        Love
                          Jesus

This little book comes straight from my heart. Each poem was written during quiet moments with God—times when I felt His love most clearly. My hope is that as you read, you'll feel Him walking beside you too, reminding you that you're never alone.

About the Author

Jane Wyman is a lifelong resident of Pennsylvania. She is a creative, fun loving and very determined person. Her pastimes are camping, painting, flower arranging, swimming, fishing and crafts. She also enjoys collecting snow globes, teddy bears and pinecones and writes poetry. Her favorite pastime is taking a cup of coffee to the park, writing poetry in God's creation.

www.ingramcontent.com/pod-product-compliance
Lightning Source LLC
Chambersburg PA
CBHW030558080526
44585CB00012B/420